EMBRACING THE
PROPHETS
IN CONTEMPORARY CULTURE

Walter Brueggemann
on Confronting Today's "Pharaohs"

A 6-SESSION STUDY BY WALTER BRUEGGEMANN WITH TIM SCORER

Morehouse Education Resources,
a division of Church Publishing Incorporated
Editorial Offices: 600 Grant Street, Suite 630, Denver, CO 80203

For catalogs and orders call:
1-800-242-1918
www.ChurchPublishing.org

ISBN-13: 978-1-60674-092-7

"I can't imagine a more important set of biblical texts to study in our day and age than the Old Testament Prophets, and I can't imagine a better teacher than Walter Brueggemann, a modern-day prophet himself! This is a wonderful multi-media resource, well-designed to help all of us who are Christians to better engage the power of the prophets for our own cultural context. Highly recommended!"

—Brent A. Strawn
Candler School of Theology,
Emory University

"The next best thing to having Walter Brueggemann, the premier biblical scholar of our generation, lead your small-group study! *Embracing the Prophets* is a marvelous resource for all who are interested in a provocative and penetrating conversation about the ancient text and the dominant forces of contemporary culture."

—Louis Stulman
Professor of Religion,
University of Findlay
Co-author of You are My People:
An Introduction to Prophetic Literature

"A marvelous opportunity—for an individual or a whole church—to learn not only about the way the ancient prophets can be heard to speak to our time but about religious teaching more generally. Don't miss it!"

—James Boyd White
*Hart Wright Professor of Law emeritus
and Professor of English emeritus
University of Michigan
Author of* Connecting to the Gospel

"What a gift to local faith communities this series is! In it Walter Brueggemann brings a wealth of scholarly study on the prophets to life in an accessible, thematic fashion that engages our minds even as it also challenges our living. From the Mosaic covenant in Exodus to Isaiah's cry of "Comfort my people," Brueggemann takes us on a journey through prophetic witness that breaks through our culture of denial, mourns our public failures, and ultimately gives us hope in God's re-creative vision. The study guide provides a treasure trove of discussion ideas, and the conversations among participants in the videos are provocative. This is biblical study at its best."

—Leonora Tubbs Tisdale
*Clement-Muehl Professor of Homiletics
Yale Divinity School*

"Embracing the Prophets is a remarkable gift to everyone interested in the Israelite prophets and their significance for contemporary faith. The series weds the always compelling, deeply relevant and clear teaching of Walter Brueggemann with thought-provoking group reflections and helpful study questions. The result is a richly substantive, accessible exploration of these 'strange' ancient voices and what it means to heed their persistent call for covenant fidelity in our own time."

—Christine Roy Yoder
Associate Professor of Old Testament Language, Literature and Exegesis
Columbia Theological Seminary

"Embracing the Prophets in Contemporary Culture" is a perfect tool for study, reflection and community building. The ever-moving and provocative Walter Brueggemann sets out prophetic thinking in clear and appealing terms as challenges to ancient cultures and worlds. Then he turns to our contemporary western world and finds an urgent prophetic call to resist consumerism and power structures that oppress and dehumanize us all. Brueggemann is at his passionate best, but there is even more here—a model of communal study in which the participants contribute insight and probing questions. Small group reflection is at the heart of the enterprise. This project not only instructs but shows how."

—Kathleen M. O'Connor
Professor of Old Testament, emerita
Columbia Theological Seminary

TABLE OF CONTENTS

QUICK GUIDE TO THIS HANDBOOK

TEN things to know as you begin to work with this resource:

1. HANDBOOK + WORKBOOK

This handbook is a guide to the group process as well as a workbook for everyone in the group.

2. A SIX-SESSION RESOURCE

Each of the six sessions presents a distinct topic for focused group study and conversation.

3. DVD-BASED RESOURCE

The teaching content in each session comes in the form of input by Walter Brueggemann and response by members of a small group; just over 30 minutes in length. A DVD Table of Contents is included to enable you to go directly to the beginning of each session.

4. EVERYONE GETS EVERYTHING

The handbook addresses everyone in the group, not one group leader. There is no separate "Leader's Guide."

5. GROUP FACILITATION

We based this resource on the understanding that someone will be designated as group facilitator for each session. You may choose the same person or a different person for each of the six sessions.

6. TIME FLEXIBILITY

Each of the six sessions is flexible and can be between one hour and two or more hours in length.

7. BUILD YOUR OWN SESSION

Each of the six sessions offers you four to five OPTIONS for building your own session.

8. WITHIN EACH OPTION

Most of the options feature a mixture of quotations from Walter Brueggemann and the video participants, plus questions for discussion. Some options also offer additional creative activities.

9. BEFORE THE SESSION

Each session opens with five questions for participants to consider as preparation for the session or to consider after the session.

10. CLOSING AS IF IT MATTERS

Each session concludes with a prayer written by Walter Brueggemann that emerges naturally from the content of the session.

BEYOND THE "QUICK GUIDE"

Helpful information and guidance for anyone using this resource:

1. HANDBOOK + WORKBOOK

This handbook is a guide to the group process as well as a workbook for everyone in the group.

- We hope the handbook gives you all the information you need to feel confident in shaping the program to work for you and your fellow group members.
- The work space provided in the handbook encourages you...
    — to respond to leading questions.
    — to write or draw your own reflections.
    — to note the helpful responses of other group members.

2. SIX-SESSION RESOURCE

This resource presents Walter Brueggemann insights on the prophets framed as six distinct topics of study:

1. Moses, Pharaoh, the Prophets and Us
2. The Prophets as Uncredentialed Purveyors of Covenant
3. Moral Coherence in a World of Power, Money and Violence
4. The Shrill Rhetoric that Breaks Denial
5. The Grief of Loss as Divine Judgement
6. The Promissory Language that Breaks Despair

3. DVD-BASED RESOURCE

The teaching content in each session comes in the form of input by Walter Brueggemann and response by members of a small group; just over 30 minutes in length.

Walter Brueggemann's unique presentation and accessible academic authority stimulates thoughtful and heartfelt conversation among his listeners.

The edited conversations present group sharing that builds on Brueggemann's initial teaching. They are intended to present to you a model of small group interaction that is personal, respectful and engaged.

You will notice that the participants in the DVD group also become our teachers. In many cases, quotes from the group members enrich the teaching component of this resource. This will also happen in your group—you will become teachers for one another.

We hope that the DVD presentations spark conversations about those things that matter most to those who are called to be prophets in the 21st century.

4. EVERYONE GETS EVERYTHING

The handbook addresses everyone in the group, not one group leader. There is no separate "Leader's Guide."

- Unlike many small group resources, this one makes no distinction between material for the group facilitator and for the participants. Everyone has it all!
- We believe this empowers you and your fellow group members to share creatively in the leadership.

5. GROUP FACILITATION

We designed this for you to designate a group facilitator for each session. It does not have to be the same person for all six sessions, because everyone has all the material. It is, however, essential that you and the other group members are clear about who is facilitating each session. One or two people still have to be responsible for these kind of things:

- making arrangements for the meeting space (see notes on Meeting Space, p. 8)
- setting up the space to be conducive to conversations about the things that matter most
- creating and leading an opening to the session (see notes on Opening, p. 8)
- helping the group decide on which options to focus on in that session
- facilitating the group conversation for that session
- keeping track of the time

- calling the group members to attend to the standards established for the group life (see notes on Group Standards, p. 8)
- creating space in the conversation for all to participate
- keeping the conversation moving along so that the group covers all that it set out to do
- ensuring that time is taken for a satisfying closing to the session
- making sure that everyone is clear about date, location and focus for the next session
- following up with people who missed the session

6. TIME FLEXIBILITY

Each of the six sessions is flexible and can be between one hour and two or more hours in length.

We designed this resource for your group to tailor it to fit the space available in the life of the congregation or community using it. That might be Sunday morning for an hour before or after worship, two hours on a weekday evening, or 90 minutes on a weekday morning.

Some groups might decide to spend two sessions on one of the major topics. There's enough material in each of the six topics to do that. Rushing to get through more than the time comfortably allows, results in people not having the opportunity to speak about the things that matter most to them.

7. BUILD YOUR OWN SESSION

Each of the six sessions offers you from four to five OPTIONS for building your own session. How will you decide what options to use?

- One or two people might take on the responsibility of shaping the session based on what they think will appeal to the group members. This responsibility could be shared from week to week.
- The group might take time at the end of one session to look ahead and decide on the options they will cover in the next session. This could be time consuming.
- You might decide to do your personal preparation for the session (responding to the five questions), and when everyone comes together for the session, proceed on the basis of what topics interested people the most.

8. A FORMAT WITHIN EACH OPTION

Almost every option mixes quotations from the video (from Brueggemann and the other participants), along with thoughtful questions for discussion. Occasionally, options simply feature questions or other creative activities.

9. BEFORE OR AFTER THE SESSION

Each session opens with five questions for participants to consider either as they prepare for the session or as they reflect on the session afterward.

- We intend these questions to open in you some aspect of the topic under consideration in the session, which may lead you to feel more confident when addressing this question within the group or in further discussions outside the group.

- Sometimes these questions are the same as ones raised in the context of the session. They offer the opportunity for you to do some personal reflection both before and/or after engaging in the group conversation on that topic.

10. CLOSING AS IF IT MATTERS

For each session there is a final prayer—written by Walter Brueggemann—to use when closing the session.

- It's important to close well. It's like a period at the end of a sentence. People leave the session ready for whatever comes next.
- Whether you use the closing prayer or something else one of your own choosing, closing well matters.
- Another aspect of closing is evaluation. This is not included in an intentional way in the design of the sessions; however, evaluation is such a natural and satisfying thing to do that it could be included as part of the discipline of closing each session. It's as simple as taking time to respond to these questions:
  — What insights am I taking from this session?
  — What contributed to my learning?
  — What will I do differently as a result of my being here today?

POINTERS ON FACILITATION

1. Meeting Space

- Take time to prepare the space for the group. When people come into a space that has been prepared for them, they trust the hospitality, resulting in a willingness to bring the fullness of themselves into the conversation. Something as simple as playing recorded music as people arrive will contribute to this sense of "a space prepared for you."

- Think about how the space will encourage a spirit of reverence, intimacy and care. Will there be a table in the center of the circle where a candle can be lit each time the group meets? Is there room for other symbols that emerge from the group's life?

2. Opening

- In the opening session, take time to go around the circle and introduce yourselves in some way.

- Every time a group comes together again, it takes each member time to feel fully included. Some take longer than others. An important function of facilitation is to help this happen with ease, so people find themselves participating fully in the conversation as soon as possible. We designed these sessions with this in mind. Encouraging people to share in the activity proposed under *Beginning Conversation* is one way of supporting that feeling of inclusion.

- The ritual of opening might include the lighting of a candle, an opening prayer, the singing of a hymn where appropriate, and the naming of each person present.

3. Group Standards

- There are basic standards in group life that are helpful to name when a new group begins. Once they are named, you can always come back to them as a point of reference if necessary. Here are two basics:
  - — Everything that is said in this group remains in the group. (confidentiality)
  - — We will begin and end at the time agreed. (punctuality)

- Are there any others that you need to name as you begin? Sometimes standards emerge from the life of the group and need to be named when they become evident, otherwise they are just assumed.

Note: The video that accompanies this study guide depicts a live, unscripted interaction between Walter Brueggemann and a group of adults. You may, on a very few occasions, find it difficult to hear a few of the participants. We apologize for those few moments.

SESSION | 1

MOSES, PHARAOH, THE PROPHETS AND US

BEFORE OR AFTER THE SESSION

Many participants like to come to the group conversation after considering individually some of the issues that will be raised. Others like to take time following the session to do further processing. The following five reflective activities and questions are intended to open your minds, memories and emotions regarding some aspects of this session's topic. Use the space provided here to note your reflections.

What do you already know about the story of Moses, the Israelites in Egypt, Pharaoh, Sinai, the Ten Commandments and the Golden Calf? (If you want to recall the stories, then turn to the book of Exodus: chapters 1-7, 13-14, 16-17, 19-20, 32.)

Think of Pharaoh today as "the rat race," the tendency to get pulled back into a consumer culture in spite of your best intentions, and the desire to always want more. Think of God as the One who still invites us into an alternative covenant relationship based on fidelity to God. Where is your allegiance most of the time?

How's your prayer life? Does it ever include energized, even contentious engagement with God, or is it pretty innocuous and polite? What does the way you pray tell you about your knowledge of God and God's ways?

What practices do you follow (like Sabbath) that enable you to maintain at the center of your life the things that matter most to you and to God?

Where do you experience worship that does not narcoticize you, but inspires and stirs you to deal with life and death issues in a way that matters to you and to God?

Play the first part of the DVD (about 16.5 minutes), in which Walter Brueggemann lays the groundwork for the discussion which is to follow.

When you encounter a new teacher for the first time you may actually pay as much or more attention to the teacher as to the content of what the teacher is saying, especially when the teacher is one who is as dynamic and forceful at Walter Brueggemann. Share your initial impressions of Brueggemann with one another. What impact did he have on you both in his presence and in his words?

The members of the small group meeting with Walter had an opportunity to ask questions of him. If you were there, what questions would you have wanted to ask him based on his opening presentation?

Here we are in a series that focuses on the prophets of Israel, but we are beginning with events in the great narrative of Israel that took place at least 500 years earlier. Before we go on, let's take a moment to be clear about the connections between the story of Moses and the place of the prophets in the story of Israel. As a group, speak about the words and phrases in the circle below, using them as linking ideas between the age of Moses and the era of the prophets. (**Note:** If you have a large group, you might want to do this activity in pairs or groups of three, especially if people are quite new to one another and possibly intimidated by speaking in a large group.)

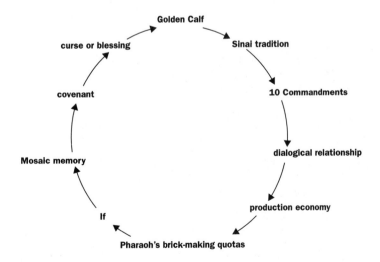

Now play the rest of Session 1. The group discussion surfaces the issues that will be covered in the rest of your session. You'll have the opportunity to choose options based on group interest and time available.

Prince asks this question of Walter:

You make the suggestion that Moses was in fact negotiating with God. I'm wondering how people today will take and process that comment? Are we really in a position to negotiate with God?

Walter responds:

That is the peculiar genius of the Jewish faith. Most of our theology comes out of Greek philosophy. When you operate in the categories of Greek philosophy there's no chance to bargain, negotiate or rap with God. It is so Jewish to be engaged in that disputatious kind of way. In Exodus 32, at the end of the Golden Calf thing, Moses really persuades God to change God's mind. This is the ground of serious prayer. Most of our prayer life is so innocuous and polite because we don't think that we have a mandate to be that seriously engaged with God.

Damon adds:

And we can be [engaged with God]. Remember the woman who kept knocking: "I'm not leaving!" and she kept knocking. And so we have to be more persistent and God will change his mind. Yea. That's good.

Later Prince adds this reflection:

Negotiation is a way of continually providing people with options as they struggle with the dilemmas of life. If anything is finalized, then that's the end. That's it. But through the process of negotiating with God, you can continually re-invent and re-invigorate and eventually reach a point where you are whole or moving in that direction.

What do you think of this more Jewish notion of negotiating with God? Have there been times when you have engaged with God in this way? Did you feel like you were negotiating with God and that there was a real possibility that God's mind would change?

Could you imagine changing your prayer life to do more "bargaining, negotiating or rapping with God"? How would you make that into a prayer practice?

Walter talks about God in this way:

> *The God of the Bible really doesn't fit our old formulations of omnipotent, omniscient and omnipresent. Omnis don't work because this is a God who is much more engaged and at risk with us in the process. That requires a different portrait of God and a different sense of ourselves as human beings and as persons of faith.*

Ariel reflects:

> *God is learning to be God by duking it out with us.*

Try testing out this notion of two visions of God by engaging with one another in a debate about the nature of God. Half the group will insist that God is "omni": all-powerful, all-seeing and all-present. God is in charge and will not be moved. The other half will speak up for a God who is malleable, willing to engage with humanity, to be changed in the process, discovering who God is by "duking it out" with us.

If you want to talk less and embody more, then use your bodies, both individually and collectively, to express the difference in these two visions of God. You could create tableaux (group compositions) with your bodies arranged to represent the difference. You could also use movement to express the two different relationships between God and us.

Whichever of these methods you use, be sure to take time to debrief afterward and identify what you learned in the process.

OPTION 3: COMMODIFICATION OR FIDELITY; YOU CHOOSE!

What does Pharaoh look like in our society? Walter responds in this way:

> *In our society, Pharaoh takes the form of the rat race, and the rat race drives us to want more, to have more and to do more. We will never make enough bricks to satisfy ourselves! It is the great seduction of a consumer economy to think that you always have to have more.*

And later in the conversation he goes on to say:

> *I think the summons is, in every way we can, to resist commodification. That's going to be different for each of us in our circumstances. I suspect one thing it means is to turn off the television. It probably means to go to the neighborhood park [to] watch sports rather than [watching] big spectator sports that are all commodification. I think it requires great intentionality to be present as a deciding, responsible agent, rather than a pawn of the ideologies that push us around.*

Joanna responds:

> *It sounds like we have commodification and then we have relationship almost as though they are opposed to each other. It reminds me of a book I read in which one person says to another, "Don't 'thing' me—don't treat me like a thing." When we commodify other people then we are cutting off the relationship. It sounds like between us and God, it is the relationship that matters.*

Walter:

> *That's exactly right. The defining ingredient of real human life is fidelity. It's not wealth, power, control, knowledge. It's fidelity. And you can see that breaking up when universities no longer have students; they have consumers. Doctors no longer have patients; they have consumers. It's re-labelling us all according to a consumer ideology. It's the death of community.*

Describe a place in your life where creeping consumer ideology has undermined relationship and fidelity? In what ways is this a concern for you? To what extent are you willing to keep paying the price?

The practice of sabbath is presented by Walter as one way for individuals, families and communities to develop resistance to a consumer-oriented society:

> *Sabbath-keeping is the regular decision to opt out of the production-consumption rat race. I think we do not have energy for neighborly relationships of fidelity unless we have something like Sabbath at the center of our lives because we are exhausted by producing and consuming. One of the things busy people like us tend to do is just to add more things on but not stop doing things that are actually contrary to the truth of our lives.*

During the conversation Walter defines Sabbath in this way:

> *A regular scheduled disciplined time in which we do not practice the values of the world which are the values of production and consumption.*

In what ways might you incorporate Sabbath-keeping into your life so as to fulfill the intention of this definition?

Let's imagine that you make some choices over the next little while to change your lifestyle so that it's more oriented to relationship and fidelity than to consumerism and commodification. Take a time jump a year into the future and write as if you are already living life from a different values base. It would sound something like this:

> *It was almost a year ago that I became really intentional about changing the amount of influence that television had in my life. I realized what an insidious presence it was, programming a consumer orientation into me, and subverting the values that I really wanted to have as the basis for my life. Cutting back TV watching to one hour a day has made a huge difference, not only in removing the insistent presence of other voices, but also in opening up time for things that really do matter to me.*

You might not want to take time during the session to do this writing. You could take it away and make time during the next few days to do it. Then share with one another at the beginning of the next session what you wrote and how it affected you.

Prince introduces the matter of worship as a place where these issues could be focused:

> I sometimes sit in church and feel the focus is so much on service and praising God and not enough on a provocative sermon that causes people to question their very practice and whether or not that practice is liberating or challenging or contributing to the institutionalization of a mind set. Where is the spiritual food that is going to help us deal with the pressures of a world that is just total assault on what we think?

Prince has opened a door into a place which is clearly much on Walter's heart and mind:

> Our meeting in worship is a life and death matter in which something is at stake. I think that very much conventional church worship is narcoticized: "There's nothing important going on here so I'll just go through the motions one more time." When in fact it is a life or death matter. Annie Dillard says that if people understood what is in fact happening in Christian worship they would wear crash helmets. To understand worship that way already requires that we break the power of the ideology of Pharaoh. Pharaoh wants us to have worship that is innocuous.

When you worship, where do you experience yourself on a continuum that goes from "innocuous/narcoticized" to "life-and-death/wear a crash helmet"?

Perhaps you've never thought of worship in the terms that Brueggemann is using. What vision of worship does he evoke in you? How might you pursue that vision if you are not experiencing it already?

The challenge that Walter Brueggemann issues to us at the end of his opening teaching is this:

> Our work in the life of the contemporary church is to continue to reflect on how we are called to live a life of dialogical covenant which is an alternative existence even though we, like ancient Israel, are always seduced out of it into other modes of existence. For the prophets, the great IF of Exodus 19 hovers over our life to see whether we will be choosing a life of blessing or a life of curse.

One thing about Walter, as you've probably already gathered—he doesn't mince words!

As a group, talk together about how you are doing in your life as an alternative faith community, knowing that other modes of existence are always trying to seduce you. Use this frame below as a way to organize your conversation:

Ways that we are choosing a life of blessing:	Ways that we are choosing a life of curse:

Offer this prayer:

> We are dazzled
> > by the way you continually reach out to us in fidelity,
> > and then reach out to us yet again.
> You reach out to us in transformative love,
> > inviting us to a new life.
> You reach out to us with sovereign commands,
> > summoning us to obedience
> > out beyond ourselves.
> You reach out to us and bind us to yourself.
>
> And we,
> > transformed by your love
> > and summoned to a new life of obedience,
> > move in and out with you.
>
> We trust and then betray;
> > we praise you and then resist;
> > we thank you and then deny.
> And you reach out!
>
> Enwrap us in the dazzling reality
> > that you make all things new,
> > even for us.
>
> *—Walter Brueggemann, Cincinnati, 2011*

SESSION 2

THE PROPHETS AS UNCREDENTIALED PURVEYORS OF COVENANT

BEFORE OR AFTER THE SESSION

Many participants like to come to the group conversation after considering individually some of the issues that will be raised. Others like to take time following the session to do further processing. The following five reflective activities and questions are intended to open your minds, memories and emotions regarding some aspects of this session's topic. Use the space provided here to note your reflections.

The prophets had a gift for seeing the world through God's eyes rather than through the eyes of the dominant culture in which they were immersed. This isn't easy, especially when you think that your welfare is totally wrapped up with the welfare of the culture. Go on a trip in your community doing nothing other than looking at the world through the eyes of God.

Pick out a book of poetry, or look for poetry in some other place like public transit or on the internet. Find a poem that shocks you into seeing the world or some aspect of it in a completely fresh way.

Take your Bible and find the books that are named after prophets. Notice one of the names standing out for you. Find out as much as you can about that prophet. What are you still wondering about that character who was destined to find a place in your life 2500 years later?

How would you identify the "zone of freedom" where you are free to be yourself quite apart from all the socio-economic pressures and requirements in which you are immersed? It's OK to say there isn't one!

Think about your church, if you have one. To what extent do you think that it has become a box that contains God and keeps God safe and domesticated? Have you heard any voices recently that are railing against this way of relating to God?

Play the first part of the DVD (about 17.5 minutes), in which Walter Brueggemann lays the groundwork for the discussion which is to follow.

After watching the first portion of the video, get comfortable, close your eyes and listen as these Brueggemann descriptors of the prophets are slowly read aloud by one member of the group. Allow yourself to get a specific picture of a prophet from the data that Walter has offered us:

- a poet
- artistically playful
- imaginal
- unaccredited
- with no prophetic training
- without social authority
- emotionally bold
- unmanageable
- naming things the way they are
- eruptive
- full of elusive metaphors and images
- an emancipated imagination
- alarming
- casting issues of fidelity and infidelity in your face
- beyond control
- abrasive
- a master of familial language
- with authority in the rhetoric
- mesmerizing
- imagining God's incredible freedom
- opening, opening, opening

and with your eyes still closed…

Listen to the words of a prophet as you get a sense of the energy and intentionality that they brought to their world. (Please read this with wild prophetic energy!)

Jeremiah 2:4-13, 20-22, 26-28

4 Hear the word of the Lord, O house of Jacob, and all the families of the house of Israel.
5 Thus says the Lord:

> What wrong did your ancestors find in me
>   that they went far from me,
> and went after worthless things, and became
>   worthless themselves?
> 6 They did not say, "Where is the Lord
>   who brought us up from the land of
>   Egypt,
> who led us in the wilderness,
>   in a land of deserts and pits
> in a land of drought and deep darkness,
>   in a land that no one passes through,
>   where no one lives?"
> 7 I brought you into a plentiful land
>   to eat its fruits and its good things.
> But when you entered you defiled my land,
>   and made my heritage an abomination.
> 8 The priests did not say, "Where is the
>   Lord?"
> Those who handle the law did not know
>   me;
> the rulers transgressed against me;
>   the prophets prophesied by Baal,
> and went after things that do not profit.

> 9 Therefore once more I accuse you,
>   says the Lord,
>   and I accuse your children's children.

¹⁰ Cross to the coasts of Cyprus and look,
    send to Kedar and examine with care;
    see if there has ever been such a thing.
¹¹ Has a nation changed its gods,
    even though they are no gods?
But my people have changed their glory
    for something that does not profit.
¹² Be appalled, O heavens, at this,
    be shocked, be utterly desolate,
                                        says the Lord,

¹³ for my people have committed two evils:
    they have forsaken me,
the fountain of living water,
    and dug out cisterns for themselves,
cracked cisterns
    that can hold no water.

²⁰ For long ago you broke your yoke
    and burst your bonds,
    and you said, "I will not serve!"
On every high hill
    and under every green tree
    you sprawled and played the whore.
²¹ Yet I planted you as a choice vine,
    from the purest stock.
How then did you turn degenerate
    and become a wild vine?
²² Though you wash yourself with lye
    and use much soap,
    the stain of your guilt is still before me,
        says the Lord God.

²⁶ As a thief is shamed when caught,
    so the house of Israel shall be shamed—
they, their kings, their officials,
    their priests, and their prophets,
²⁷ who say to a tree, "You are my father,"
    and to a stone, "You gave me birth."
For they have turned their backs to me,
    and not their faces.
But in the time of their trouble they say,
    "Come and save us!"
²⁸ But where are your gods
    that you made for yourself?
Let them come, if they can save you,
    in your time of trouble;
for you have as many gods
    as you have towns, O Judah.

With eyes open share with one another the image of the prophet that came to you. What was the emotional impact on you of this charismatic character? What new sense do you have of the prophets of Israel?

Once again get comfortable and close your eyes. Listen as these Brueggemann descriptors of the world of Solomon are slowly read aloud by one of the group. Allow yourself to get a sense of all that the word *Solomon* represents from the data that Walter has offered us:

- globalization
- world economy organized
- wealth flowing to Jerusalem
- the "golden touch" of the Old Testament
- a Biblical IMF (International Monetary Fund)
- controlling
- quantifying
- measuring
- top-down coercion
- extreme bureaucracy
- memos
- work schedules
- production quotas
- horses, chariots, slaves, wives and gold accounted for
- official-speak
- one-dimensional
- vitality of God pressed down
- God under house arrest
- elites with power
- closing, closing, closing

Now read aloud these selected verses from the first book of Kings: 6:1-7; 7:1-12 and 48-51; 10:1-13 and 23-29. Notice the energy and intentionality that is Solomon's world and that was the socio-economic context in which the prophets lived out God's call.

With eyes open, share with one another the sense of the Solomonic world that came to you. What was the emotional impact on you of this reality? What new sense do you have of who Solomon was and what he represented in the narrative of ancient Israel?

Walter presents us with this strategic question: "How do you penetrate the Solomonic world of memos?" This is the challenge of the prophets. For a period of about 250 years, no more than 20 prophets took on the challenge and achieved a significant record in the canon of scripture. Why do you think that they left such an impression not only on their moment in history, but also in the biblical narrative and the Judeo-Christian tradition?

Now play the rest of Session 2 on the DVD. The group discussion surfaces the issues that will be covered in the rest of your session together. You'll have the opportunity to choose options based on group interest and available time.

In his teaching Brueggemann makes much of the notion that the prophets of Israel were also poets:

> *We don't make nearly enough of the fact that the prophets are poets engaged in artistic playfulness that keeps opening, opening, opening, while memos and production schedules keep closing, closing, closing.*

Chris asks Walter to say some more about the reason for the prophets using the poetry of imagination. Walter responds:

> *I think that the reason the prophets speak in poetry is that they are trying by their words to sketch out the mystery of God, and what they know is that God is so hidden and so holy that no one image or phrase will catch God. So what you get is an explosion of artistic portrayals.*
>
> *They claim with the "Thus saith the Lord" that their sketching of God is given to them by God. I'm not quarreling with that except that human artistic ingenuity is certainly present in their offer of the poetry. And the poetry is revelatory. It reveals something about God that was not available until the poetry was uttered. That's what good artistry does. Good artistry shows us something that was never seen or heard until this artist does it.*

Consider the following passage of human artistic ingenuity from the prophet Micah (6:1-8). Have one group member read the passage aloud as the others listen. As you read and listen, watch for something to be revealed to you that was not evident to you before this moment.

> [1] Hear what the Lord says:
>   Rise, plead your case before
>   the mountains,
>   and let the hills hear your voice.
> [2] Hear, you mountains, the controversy of
>   the Lord,
>   and you enduring foundations of the
>   earth;
> for the Lord has a controversy with his
>   people,
>   and he will contend with Israel.
>
> [3] "O my people, what have I done to you?
>   In what have I wearied you? Answer me!
> [4] For I brought you up from the land of
>   Egypt,
>   and redeemed you from the house of
>   slavery;
> and I sent before you Moses,
>   Aaron, and Miriam.
> [5] O my people, remember now what King
>   Balak of Moab devised,
>   what Balaam son of Beor answered him,
> and what happened from Shittim to Gilgal,
>   that you may know the saving acts of the
>   Lord."
>
> [6] "With what shall I come before the Lord,
>   and bow myself before God on high?

Shall I come before him with burnt-
    offerings,
    with calves a year old?
[7] Will the Lord be pleased with thousands of
    rams,
    with tens of thousands of rivers of oil?
Shall I give my firstborn for my
    transgression,
    the fruit of my body for the sin of my
    soul?"
[8] He has told you, O mortal, what is good;
    and what does the Lord require of you
but to do justice, and to love kindness,
    and to walk humbly with your God?

Read the passage a second time, continuing to be attentive to what new thing you are discovering, then share your new discoveries with one another either in the whole group, in pairs or triads, depending on group size and time available.

After sharing, stand back from the text and reflect on what just happened. In what ways has it illustrated what Brueggemann was saying in the opening words of this option?

OPTION 2: NEITHER PREDICTORS NOR ACTIVISTS BUT IMAGINERS

Notice how Brueggemann in his initial teaching critiqued both conservative and liberal Christians in terms of the ways that each group has misunderstood the prophets:

> *Conservatives tend to think the prophets are predictors, predicting the future until they can predict Jesus. It's a mistake to talk as though the prophets are talking about Jesus. They are not predictors of the future.*

> *Liberals tend to interpret prophets as social activists in which their prophetic ministry is presented as righteous indignation against injustice. But they are not social activists. They rarely take sides in social questions.*

> *The prophets are imaginers, not predictors or social activists. Conservatives and liberals have been threatened by the poetry of the prophets so they have acted to make them manageable, but their number one characteristic is that they are not manageable.*

Joanna follows up this initial teaching with this challenge to Brueggemann:

> *I have to admit that I'm one of the liberals who has seen the prophets as a call to justice and you're telling me that that is as much a lack of imagination as seeing the prophets as predictors.*

Walter responds:

> *I don't want to dismiss that accent on justice because it's certainly there, but I think that if we don't see that it's cast in poetic terms that it leads to a kind of hard-nosed advocacy that becomes thinner than the poetry wants it to be.*

Joanna:

> *I'm struggling with this because I see a call for justice being pretty serious. When you talk about poetry I almost get a sense that I'm watering down the call for justice.*

Walter:

> *What I want to argue is that behind the call for justice is the articulation of God as an agent and character in the world, and justice is simply a requirement of this God who is an agent. And if God is not an agent and a character, then justice just becomes a human idea rather than a divine mandate. So my sequence of thinking about this is the Sinai covenant saying that you are obligated to do these things. Then 500 years later, through this poetry, the God of Sinai shows up in fresh ways to make this claim again, but because the ideology of Solomon is so forceful, they have to find new rhetorical strategies to penetrate that ideology.*

> *The reason this seems important to me is that I think the same thing is true in our society. I believe that the ideology of national militarism and the market is so powerful that you can't just butt against it, but you have to penetrate your way through it to reach people at a deeper level. And that's why I think the artistic is so terribly important.*

Joanna:

> *So the artistic is a subversive act?*

Walter:

> *That's right. It subverts the dominant ideology.*

What's your response to the important case that Brueggemann is making for seeing the prophets as strategic imaginers and not as predictors of the future or hard-nosed social activists?

Talk about some of the places where you are aware, in the past or in the present, of artistic imaginers living out a divine mandate by penetrating the dominant ideology through the wild potency of their artistry. (**Note:** For two possible examples to help group members get started, consider visiting this web link: *http://en.wikipedia.org/wiki/Tomoko_Uemura_in_Her_Bath* [here is the link to the actual photo: *http://www.masters-of-photography.com/S/smith/smith_minamata.html*] or the words to Harry Chapin's song "The Shortest Story," *http://www.sing365.com/music/lyric.nsf/The-Shortest-Story-lyrics-Harry-Chapin/E85088E70701145148256CAA002EB5C7.*)

As you think strategically and faithfully, where could you imagine letting loose artistic playfulness to subvert some expression of the dominant ideology of this day?

Damon asks:

> *In order to enact this artistic playfulness (of the prophets) in this modern time, would we have to become ascetics or hermits?*

Walter's first response is a general statement that provides a guideline for each one of us to consider as we wonder about our own capacity to live more prophetically:

> *We have to maintain a zone of freedom in our lives that says our life is not completely co-opted by the market ideology.*

But then Walter takes the opportunity (in responding to a black preacher) to reflect on the prophetic role of the black church in America:

> *What I'm describing is what black preachers have done best. Black worship and black preaching is kind of this imaginative zone. If I understand it rightly, the reason the black church has historically been so important is that it was a zone of freedom from the control of the white master. And so you could engage in this artistic probe of stuff that didn't have to answer to the reason of the plantation owners. It's a nice analog for what I was saying about Solomon and poetry in downtown Jerusalem.*

> *I do believe that the really important church question now is how to maintain that zone of freedom where we can articulate the world differently.*

What is the zone of freedom in your life that says your life is not completely co-opted by the market ideology?

If that zone is either non-existent or too small for you to breath and take action, how might you go about expanding and clarifying it?

OPTION 4: INSIDE, OUTSIDE AND UPSIDE DOWN

Walter says to us:

I think that prophetic poetry is almost always going to come from outsiders because insiders, people who are tenured like me, have too much at stake in accommodating ideology. So it always comes from the edges, I think. And the astonishing thing is that the poetry from the edges got into our sacred book because over time it was known to be unavoidable.

Alice responds:

It's hard to see the edges when there are so many boxes that we've built. I was thinking about this when you said that Solomon built God a house where God couldn't move, and I'm remembering, obviously a bit later historically, that John says, "The Word became flesh and pitched its tent with us." I've always been fascinated with the nomadic tradition of the Israelites. When they settle down, they build the city and this temple, and they're all crushed when the temple gets destroyed. I don't want to lessen the sadness and the grief of that moment and that part of the tradition, but listening to what you're talking about, this may have been one of the best things that happened to the Israelites. Their box was destroyed and the diaspora was in fact a bit of a gift.

Walter:

Even though it didn't feel like it. I'm just astonished then to think that every time the local congregation meets around these texts it is an opportunity for risky emancipatory speech even though every congregation has

very vigilant censors to make sure nothing like this is ever said, but it does get said because these texts are just incredibly generative.

Joanna:

But what happens then if the church becomes the box and then someone outside the church may need to be that voice?

Walter:

That's exactly right. That's where we are. I would say that the institutional church in our culture has largely become a box that contains God so that we need to be watching and listening for who the poetic imaginers are that are truth-tellers among us or beyond us.

What box are you in, individually and as a community of faith? In what ways are you the guardians of a box that contains God?

Is it too risky to name the boxes of your congregation? Where are you aware of the "very vigilant censors" making sure that the "risky emancipatory speech" is never uttered?

Ariel reflects:

> When you were talking about the prophets making God strange; it's about capturing our attention. I feel that we are wanting to know more about this strange other and we are also discovering new things about ourselves, so there's a motion, questing to figure out who we are becoming and who God is becoming. It's not a staying in place thing.

Walter:

> In a time of anxiety like our time there is a great temptation in the church to want to offer certitudes and find answers and closure. That is idolatrous every time. The poetic force of the prophets in their imagination keeps refusing certitude by opening up another line of thought and emotion.

Tim:

> There's an unpredictability of the prophet's voice.

Walter:

> You never know when a poem will erupt!

Tim:

> That seems like a feature of this work.

Damon:

> Now here's a deal! We fell into a kind of lurch after King (MLK) died. Everybody was waiting for a new prophetic voice, a new King, instead of everyone rising up and becoming a prophetic voice. Come

> from within you! Do that which you know to be right! You don't always need a crowd. You'd be surprised if you have the guts and fortitude to say it. You could be developing a crowd to follow you!

Where are you hearing poems erupt that are irresistible to you?

What are you learning about God? What is God learning about God?

How's your courage these days?

Offer this prayer:

We live our lives in tight little boxes
    with high edges and sharp corners.
Or we live day after day,
           endlessly,
               without focus or aim.

And then,
    in the middle of our boxes
    and our randomness,
your presence
      explodes us
         and we must decide again about our lives.

You come to us
    in poetic utterance,
    in artistic sketch,
    in revolutionary image.

You engage us by the way you dispatch your faithful artists,
    old time prophets
    and contemporary truth-sayers,
        the ones who show us our deathliness,
        the ones who imagine us
        to a new life congruent with your own life.

By your spirit
    open us to such ancient possibility
        beyond our fear and beyond our pride.

Come good spirit,
    come in utterance,
    come in sketch,
    come in image,
    come in all the ways that seep through our certitude,
        our management,
        and our self-importance.
Come, good spirit!

—Walter Brueggemann, Cincinnati, 2011

SESSION | 3

MORAL COHERENCE IN A WORLD OF POWER, MONEY AND VIOLENCE

BEFORE OR AFTER THE SESSION

Many participants like to come to the group conversation after considering individually some of the issues that will be raised. Others like to take time following the session to do further processing. The following five reflective activities and questions are intended to open your minds, memories and emotions regarding some aspects of this session's topic. Use the space provided here to note your reflections.

"We have to maintain a zone of freedom in our lives that says our life is not completely co-opted by the market ideology." Watch for times during the week when you have a clear sense of living in that zone of freedom. Notice what it's like to be there and what makes it challenging to stay there. See if you have a practice that enables you to go to that zone to be replenished, sustained and inspired.

As you go through the week, watch for places where you are living the great *if*. You might experience it as "*If* I do this _____, then the *consequence* will be this _____." Or you might notice it more as "Because I have taken these actions, *therefore* this has followed as a consequence." Notice also what considerations you bring to each choice you make.

Watch for places of imagination and artistry that are powerful enough to subvert the dominant culture of commodification, consumerism, profit, militarism and violence. How do you know that these people of playful imagination are penetrating the bubble of Solomon's world? What are the signs?

"I would say that the institutional church in our culture has largely become a box that contains God so that we need to be watching and listening for who the poetic imaginers are that are truth-tellers among us or beyond us." What experiences of "Church-in-a-box" are you having this week? Have you noticed any poetic imaginers or truth-tellers that might be allies for you in getting things "out of the box"?

Open one of your Bibles to one of the prophets and try out your prophetic voice! These passages deserve to be read with the full weight of the righteous anger, indignation and poetic fervor of the prophet poet. These are no meek offerings! The prophets were willing to put their lives on the line to have God heard. See what that feels like when you begin to embody the prophets!

ESSENTIAL 1: HEARING THE WORDS OF A CONTEMPORARY PROPHET

Play the first part of the DVD (about 17.5 minutes), in which Walter Brueggemann lays the groundwork for the discussion which is to follow.

Let's be clear about the main points that Brueggemann is making in his initial presentation:

- The prophets through their poetry insist that there is a moral coherence in the world.
- These prophetic poets were writing poetry and preaching in a society that ignored the notion of moral order in favor of a socio-economic order that benefitted the urban elite in Jerusalem at the expense of the rural peasants.
- When things are set up in this way you will inevitably get a society of violence.
- We live in such a world today where there are huge concentrations of power, money and control and in which violence is increasingly normative.
- The prophets remind people of the claims of the Sinai Covenant which has at its center the "if " relationship with God: *if* you obey my commandments, *then* you will have a good life.
- The Book of Deuteronomy, in its meditation on the ten commandments, insists that there is moral accountability and that choices have consequences which cannot be evaded no matter how powerful or wealthy you are.
- The word *therefore* is the lynch pin in the relationship between choice and consequence: "*Because* you have done so and so, *therefore* I will..."
- The way to make the world work is to keep the covenantal relationship with

God; the way to destroy it is to violate that relationship.

- The prophets invite their listeners to step outside the ideology of money, power, control and violence as though the future of the world depends on our following the covenantal agreement.
- The poet prophets do not make contemporary diagnoses or predictions but they do feed our imaginations to think about moral accountability in all areas of our living including our relationship with creation.
- We cannot live with impunity in a world where we are commanded by covenantal obligations. Eventually a society that violates the moral center and turns away from a covenantal relationship with God is going to pay for it.
- The prophets insist that the maintenance of public life depends on neighborly fidelity.

These 12 points are offered in an attempt to summarize the essential elements of Brueggemann's initial presentation. Is anything missing?

Before going on, take a moment to review the list and to add other points from his presentation that seem important to you as a small group.

Why does all this matter? How does this get me in touch with my own experience and what small, next step I can take?

Hear the words of the two prophets to which Brueggemann made reference in his presentation, Micah and Jeremiah. When these passages are read aloud, they need to be read with the full weight of the righteous anger, indignation and poetic fervor of the prophet poet. The prophets were willing to put their lives on the line to have God heard. They were speaking truth to the massive power of an economic system that favored those who would be only too ready to crush an upstart, unaccredited poet! Are there any in the group who would be willing to read with that kind of chaotic energy?

As you read and listen, notice the "If… therefore" construction to which Walter refers.

Micah 3:9-12

[9] Hear this, you rulers of the house of Jacob
   and chiefs of the house of Israel,
      who abhor justice
      and pervert all equity,
[10] who build Zion with blood
   and Jerusalem with wrong!
[11] Its rulers give judgment for a bribe,
   its priests teach for a price,
   its prophets give oracles for money;
      yet they lean upon the Lord and say,
      "Surely the Lord is with us!
      No harm shall come upon us."
[12] Therefore because of you
   Zion shall be ploughed as a field;
Jerusalem shall become a heap of ruins,
   and the mountain of the house a
      wooded height.

Jeremiah 7:8-15

[8] Here you are, trusting in deceptive words to no avail. [9] Will you steal, murder, commit adultery, swear falsely, make offerings to Baal, and go after other gods that you have not known, [10] and then come and stand before me in this house, which is called by my name, and say, 'We are safe!'—only to go on doing all these abominations? [11] Has this house, which is called by my name, become a den of robbers in your sight? You know, I too am watching, says the Lord. [12] Go now to my place that was in Shiloh, where I made my name dwell at first, and see what I did to it for the wickedness of my people Israel. [13] And now, because you have done all these things, says the Lord, and when I spoke to you persistently, you did not listen, and when I called you, you did not answer, [14] therefore I will do to the house that is called by my name, in which you trust, and to the place that I gave to you and to your ancestors, just what I did to Shiloh. [15] And I will cast you out of my sight, just as I cast out all your kinsfolk, all the offspring of Ephraim.

Now play the rest of Session 3 on the DVD. The group discussion surfaces the issues that will be covered in the rest of your session together. You'll have the opportunity to choose options based on group interest and available time.

We want to develop further our understanding that *these prophets are poets and artists, not scientists.* They are *poets engaged in artistic playfulness.* They are *masters of human artistic ingenuity,* trying by their words to sketch out the mystery of God even though they know that God is so hidden and so holy that no one image or phrase will catch God. Through their wrestling with language and image *they manage to reveal things about God that were not available until the poetry was uttered.*

Further to the teaching of Session 2, Brueggemann adds these ways of thinking about these prophetic poets:

- Remember, the prophets are not presenting scientific syllogisms (logical arguments with conclusions inferred from propositions). *No, these are acts of artistic imagination.*
- They are invitations to step outside the ideology of money, power, control and violence and *entertain the world in another way,* as though the world were a covenantal agreement that depends on keeping certain commandments.
- The poetry says that *when you violate* the commandments *you will destroy creation.*
- *It's hung together simply by a poetic, "therefore."*
- There is no way to translate the poetic presentation into scientific argument, except that if you bring to the poetry something like global warming, you can make the case that the violation of the moral limits of God's creation helps produce an environment where it is increasingly unlivable. I'm not suggesting that you can take these ancient poems and transpose them into contemporary diagnoses, *but what these poems do is feed our imagination to think about moral*

accountability according to the claims of the Sinai covenant even though you cannot apply them one on one.

- It's not sociological analysis (even though well-informed); it's a tease to ask if we look carefully at the way we are doing our policy formation. What do you think the outcomes and consequences of that are going to be? Because you cannot live with impunity in a world where you are commanded by covenantal obligations.

Given that background to this literary form and to the intention of the poets, take this passage from the prophet Hosea and identify the way that it exemplifies what is being described:

Hosea 4:1-3

¹ Hear the word of the Lord, O people of Israel;
  for the Lord has an indictment against the inhabitants of the land.
There is no faithfulness or loyalty,
  and no knowledge of God in the land.
² Swearing, lying, and murder,
  and stealing and adultery break out;
  bloodshed follows bloodshed.
³ Therefore the land mourns,
  and all who live in it languish;
together with the wild animals
  and the birds of the air,
    even the fish of the sea are perishing.

Ariel responds enthusiastically to Walter's initial presentation:

> It's really good news; another way that God is on our side if we are trying to do something life-giving. God really is on all our sides!

When you think about it, Ariel is really expressing the essence of moral coherence in her own spontaneous way. In response, Walter goes on to expand on his initial presentation:

> When we try to interpret these texts, what we have to work at is to deliver them from an escapist supernaturalism as though God is a big guy in the sky that's going to sweep in. That's not what they're talking about. What they're talking about is that these ways of organizing social power contain within themselves the seeds of death. They use supernatural language because they're trying to keep it in the frame of reference of the Sinai Covenant where God is a real agent. So they understand the agency of God, but it's not the agency of God that is outside the processes of socio-economic history.

> If you stay inside the context of the Old Testament, it did turn out that Jerusalem was destroyed. The poetic tradition insists that Jerusalem was not destroyed because Babylon was an aggressor; Jerusalem was destroyed because God couldn't put up with it anymore. If you read on in the Old Testament that was not the end of the story, but it is a very weighty moment in which right down to the destruction there were narcoticized people in Jerusalem who believed this will never happen to them because they are God's people. But the prophets rather relentlessly say, "You don't get a pass for that. You get yours too." So that the "if" of Mount Sinai is really sturdy and durable in the experience of the Old Testament up to the destruction (of the Temple). If you read past that in the Old Testament, then God circles back with forgiveness, but it's not a cheap grace. It's a very hard, demanding grace.

Alice then affirms:

> So essentially there are consequences, but that's not the end of the story.

Walter:

That's right, except that when you get the consequences you don't know that it's not the end of the story. I think there is this profound contradiction in Biblical faith between moral symmetry and the move beyond moral symmetry, but that's the way it is in all our serious relationships. We do not in fact say to our spouse, for example, "I will love you no matter what." What we say is, "It's your turn to take out the garbage, God damn it! You've got to do that if you want the relationship to work." Now, if you fail to take out the garbage enough times it may be that the answer will be, "That's all right, you don't have to take the garbage out." Or it may be, "I won't put up with this anymore. You've got to take it out." That's the crisis of fidelity that these poets are always processing. Each time it is not known ahead of time. You can argue in the big story it is known ahead of time, but each time it is not known ahead of time.

What we have woven through this conversation is an exploration of some of the key theological questions of any age, 21st century BCE or 21st century CE. In the great unfolding of God's Time, a mere flash!

Your task as a group is to re-read the conversation above and name the deep truths that emerge from it for you. It's in the wrestling with text, whether in the Bible or in the conversations around the Bible that insight emerges. It's all about discernment and revelation!

Conduct the following activity done either in the whole group or in small groups of three or four members each.

Imagine that you are any one of the key players in the drama of relationship that is presented by Walter Brueggemann. Try getting inside the experience and motivation of each one by speaking for them:

- one of the prophet poets who is part of the urban scene

- Solomon, the builder of the Jerusalem Temple, the architect of the socio-economic order

- another prophet, but one who comes from a rural setting

- a member of the wealthy Jerusalem elite

What new insights come as a result of speaking into the identity of each of these characters in the drama of ancient Israel?

Walter:

> *I think the key point is that we must discover that what we think to be a given world is in fact a constructed ideology. It's not given. If it's given, I have no options. If it's constructed I can opt otherwise. It seems to me that the Christian gospel is always an invitation to "otherwise" away from the ideology that has the force of givenness. But, of course our churches, by and large, have a sense that they do not want the ideology named as an ideology. They'd rather think it's a given.*

Ariel carries this reflection into a specific situation that most of us have experienced in our lifetime:

> *It's so great that in our lifetime we got to see the alternative understanding of reality: the overthrow of Apartheid in South Africa without violence. We were witnesses to that. We were witnesses to de Klerk being cornered into behaving much better than he expected to behave.*

Chris:

> *So it takes a person or a group of people expressing that outwardly to make it happen.*

Walter:

> *That's right. And that group we sometimes name "the church."*

Joanna:

> *But sometimes the church houses the comfortable.*

Ariel:

> *But then we get to see the Dutch Reformed Church repent in South Africa and we get to see "Truth and Reconciliation."*

The prophets saw it as their vocation and unavoidable responsibility to identify as clearly as they could the constructed ideologies that the wealthy and the powerful wanted to keep naming as "given." As long as there was a general presumption that the system was given and unchangeable, everything was frozen in place. Ariel has offered one very prominent global example of a time when an ideological system was brought down nonviolently. What other specific examples can you name of this dynamic in action either globally, nationally or locally?

Joanna calls the group back to the matter of the "if" that Walter raised in the first session:

> We continue to neglect the "ifs" even now. It seems that when we do that, it's not that God is punishing us, it's that, inherently, because of the way God made the world, it's an unsustainable situation. So in a way it comes upon us not as a punishment we don't deserve, but as a part of the way God made the world. It's unsustainable because we create the injustice that we have in this world of power and inequality.

Prince continues:

> One of the difficulties in resolving some of these issues is our own way of thinking about our relationship with other people where we acknowledge our own complicity in creating the mindset of some people who see us as their enemies. So we feel this compulsion to defend ourselves (which I can understand) but without ever acknowledging that some people have legitimate grievances against us and our foreign policy kinds of ideas. We've got to examine ourselves before we can begin to judge others, and we don't do that well.

Joanna:

> I think that our prayers, especially in church, become ways of excusing ourselves so that we say, "We pray for the poor and the helpless" and we think that lets us off the hook. We don't have to do anything now because we've prayed for them. If we just pray for the poor and let it go at that and leave the church thinking we're just fine, I think we become the maintainers of that system and we still uphold it even when we think we're not. It makes us hypocritical.

Alice:

> You speak of consequences for our not obeying covenant at the same time when we do speak prophetically and act prophetically there are consequences to that as well. That's perhaps why we don't speak and act prophetically.

Joanna:

> Jesus said once that if you are going to live the life of the kingdom you've got to be prepared to be crucified. And lots of us aren't prepared. If it's threatening and it's scary, a lot of churches don't want to do that. We also don't want to give up anything we have for the common good.

As you listen to the members of the group reflecting on the personal implications of Walter's teaching on the prophets, you hear them struggling with the nature of their own participation in the dominant culture and the choices they make in the face of that and in response to the call of the prophets. Recall when Walter said this: *What the prophets are talking about is that these ways of organizing social power contain within themselves the seeds of death.* When we begin to look at our own involvement in this ideological construct we have to be able to speak honestly about the ways we are sowing and nurturing the seeds of death. Take time to do that together, recognizing that it is a sacred confessional practice and not one to take lightly.

Offer this prayer:

We run harder to win.
We work harder to break even.
We piece our lives together
          one cubit at a time,
              and we are left weary by our anxiety.
And then, in the midst of our fatigue,
    come your sovereign commandments.
We are made mindful
    that you are the glue
        that connects our present and our future.
You are the link
    that makes continuity between our choices and our destinies,
        between our much striving and our inescapable outcomes.
And we,
    shocked by your relentless, uncompromising coherence,
        break from our idols
        and slouch toward the neighborhood where you will us to be.

We are felled into a company of brothers and sisters
    who care for us and
    who call us to care,
    neighbors all.
We find open air
    and free space
    and safe companions
        whereby we may quit running
            and working
            and exhausting.
We fall back into our simplicity,
    faithful to you and to neighbors,
just as you command us.

—*Walter Brueggemann, Cincinnati, 2011*

JEREMIAH

...rds of Jeremiah son of Hilkiah, of the priests who were in Anathoth in the land of Benjamin, 2 to whom the word of the LORD came in the days of King Josiah son of Amon of Judah, in the thir- teenth year of his reign. 3 It came also in the days of Jehoiakim son of Josiah of Judah, until the end of the eleventh year of Zedekiah son of Josiah of Judah, until the captivity of Jerusalem in ... RD came to me

5 "Before I formed you in the womb I knew you, and before you were born I consecrated you; I appointed you a prophet to the nations." 6 Then I said, "Ah, Lord GOD! Truly I do not know how to speak, for I am only a boy." 7 But the LORD said to me, "Do not say, 'I am only a boy'; for you shall go to all to whom I send you,

24 And ... dead bodie... belled against... die; their fire sh... they shall be an abho...

l Gk Syr. Heb lacks *know*
it is
n Gk: Heb Pul

SESSION | 4

THE SHRILL RHETORIC THAT BREAKS DENIAL

BEFORE OR AFTER THE SESSION

Many participants like to come to the group conversation after considering individually some of the issues that will be raised. Others like to take time following the session to do further processing. The following five reflective activities and questions are intended to open your minds, memories and emotions regarding some aspects of this session's topic. Use the space provided here to note your reflections.

Watch out for poets who are speaking to you from the margins of our society. Listen to them; perhaps even collect some striking pieces of their work and bring them with you.

The dominant ideology does not want you to come to consciousness. It wants you to be a shopper, a spectator and a consumer, because when you become conscious you are not so easily administered. Pay attention. Notice the times when you break free from the grip of the dominant culture. How does that feel: exhilarating, frightening, liberating, regretful, mischievous, subversive, powerful?

Sit with the seventh chapter of Amos and notice what impact it has on you. First of all read this note from Brueggemann's teaching this week: *This is a very dramatic confrontation. Amos has just recited a poetic oracle in which he says that the northern state of Israel and the capital city and the family of the king are going to be in big trouble. Then he meets the high priest at the royal sanctuary in Bethel. The high priest—who is like the hired gun of the economic establishment—says to Amos: "You can't talk that way here. You cannot recite that poetry here because this is the king's sanctuary where never is heard a discouraging word." Then he says to Amos, "If you have to talk that kind of poetry, please go somewhere else and do it."* Okay, now read the text.

Pay attention this week to the kind of messages you receive from the world around you about how to be in relation to your body and everything about it: diet, exercise, health, sexuality, fashion and so on. When do you feel truly connected to your body? When do you feel disconnected? What's the consequence of that disconnection? What do you do to stay faithful to your body?

In preparation for the session, read the 12 quotes from Walter Brueggemann in the following section (Essential: Getting Down and Dirty, p. 51), noticing the ones that seem to resonate with you today.

Play the first part of the DVD (about 20 minutes) in which Walter Brueggemann lays the groundwork for the discussion which is to follow.

Read some or all of these 12 quotes from the teaching and then identify the ones that have particular impact on you. What is the source of their impact? What would you want to ask Walter Brueggemann having heard his teaching and read these quotes?

- *You can't whiz through the prophets. You can't summarize them or reduce their message to a formulation. Hearing the prophets is more like attending a poetry reading. You hear the poetry read and then you have to sit with it, follow the rhetoric, watch for the images and phrases, and notice the new world that emerges out of that poetry.*

- *The prophets lived in a culture of acute denial and they had to have rhetorical means and strategies to try to penetrate the denial so that their listeners could begin to get in touch with what was really going on in their lives. The reason for us to pay attention to that work is that we live in a culture of acute denial in which we do not really want to know what is happening to us or what we are doing to ourselves.*

- *The collage of king, dynasty and temple liturgy produced a sense that the chosen people Israel were immune to the risks of history and therefore nothing bad was going to happen to them and therefore no need to worry: "I tell you, do not be anxious; everything will be alright!"*

- *This ideology of being safe because we are God's people gets translated in US culture in what we call US exceptionalism; that is, that we are not subject to the rules of history because we are the chosen people in the modern world to carry democracy and all these neat things around.*

- *The crisis of 9/11 has a symbolic force among us that is completely disproportionate to what in fact happened to the Twin Towers. That was bad enough, but it wasn't that bad. What was bad was the symbolic level of awareness that we now are subject to the same violent vulnerability that everyone else in the world is.*

- *This poetry tries to subvert the ideology and get through the sense of conditionality so that people begin to notice that our lives really are in deep jeopardy and to ask what that means and what to do about it and how can we change our attitudes and our behavior and our policies in light of the impending dangers into which we have brought our society.*

- *The poetry of subversion doesn't have any meaning or any power unless we are aware of the ideology that tries to silence the poetry and ignore it. The force of the ideology always wants to silence the poets because the poets remind us of what's going on underneath the surface of our life to which we have considerable resistance.*

- *This poetry is inviting us to imagine our world differently as though the demands, the gifts and the risks of God were real in our lives.*

- *This kind of poem is useful to us because many people are experiencing our world being undone, moving at a rapid pace into a formless frightening chaos and we don't know how to cope with it. This kind of prophetic poetry can help us at emotional and interpretive levels to embrace the truth of what is going on around us. If we don't do that we look for scapegoats, we get shrill and ideological, blame people and eventually commit to violence. What the poetry says is go underneath all that and listen to these words, and these words will give you access to the stuff where you had not thought to go.*

- *None of that tells you what to do, but it asks you to notice the underneath stuff of our common life to which we don't want to pay attention because it is too scary and it's too unbearable. What the poets believe is that people who are truthful before the Lordship of God are obligated to get down and dirty about what's going on in our lives.*

- *This poetry is an offer to see the world differently. I suggest that the church colludes with much of the denial of American exceptionalism. We collude in our imagining that we are God's people and that we are safe from all this kind of stuff. What poets know is that the practitioners of the ideology always learn too late.*

- *The poet believes that if you pay attention, it's not too late yet to learn, but you've got to let the poetry come inside the ideology with its transformative power. I find that to be an incredible challenge.*

Now play the rest of Session 4 on the DVD. The group discussion surfaces the issues that will be covered in the rest of your session together. You'll have the opportunity to choose options based on group interest and available time.

OPTION 1: POETS: RECEIVING, WRITING AND RISKING

Walter:

> As you know we're never never without poets.

Damon:

> There's always somebody that God has left. Elijah had to find that out. "I'm the only one left." "No, you're not the only one left." There are many left but we just have to find the voices.

Walter:

> I get around to a lot of churches. I'm hardly ever at a church where after the meeting somebody doesn't come up to me and give me a poem they just wrote. People are writing poems everywhere. They're not very visible. They're not circulated much but the stuff is working.

> Every good poem ought to evoke more poems because, as you know, poetry tends to be generated among the outsiders so what we call third-world contexts are now seed beds for much of the emancipatory poetry that's available to us.

Chris:

> How would you say that a poem is delivered? To an individual?

Walter:

> I think people would say this just came to me and I wrote it down. I've been thinking this; I've been feeling that. I think very often people like that say, "I didn't produce the poem. I received the poem." Of course, that's what these old prophets said: "This was given to me." Jeremiah among them says, "No, no, I don't want it. You keep your words. I don't want your words." Because they're too hard.

Joanna:

> But it's risky. I think we live in a culture where we see people like Ezekiel who write poems are thought of as crackpots and we're afraid to say anything because we might be thought of as crackpots too. If we start talking about the culture and critiquing it people will say we're socialists or something worse.

Walter:

> Jeremiah was called a traitor. Worse a traitor than a crackpot!

Chris:

> So who are our modern poets and what are they saying?

Where are your poets? Who among you passes along your poems to people like Walter?

Chris ends with a question: "Who are our modern poets?" meaning the prophetic poets of our time. Notice that we have added a page (55) here of some of the poets named by the members of this group in Cincinnati. Who would you say are the prophetic poets of our time that we all need to be paying attention to?

If you really give credence to what Walter and the others are saying, you'd want to go out of your way to encourage and support your poetic voices wherever they are, most likely out in the margins. Are there some ways you could do that?

MODERN AND CONTEMPORARY POETS WITH A PROPHETIC PERSPECTIVE

Walter Brueggemann and members of the Cincinnati group make recommendations of poetic writing:

From Walter:

- Wendell Berry's poem *The Mad Farmer*, in which he is basically saying, "Be contrary. Go against the grain. Don't give in."
- And the poetry of Daniel Berrigan in which he paraphrases the biblical poets in contemporary phrasing. He's also saying that we are choosing unbearable futures for ourselves.

From Alice:

- When you read Kurt Vonnegut Junior's *Slaughterhouse-Five* (1969), you recognize Truth with a capital T.

From Prince:

- Martin Luther King's book, *Where Do We Go from Here: Chaos or Community?* which is his analysis of American race relations and the state of the movement after a decade of civil rights efforts.
- *Huckleberry Finn* by Mark Twain
- Herman Melville's poetry is subversive but you have to think to get at his deeper meaning; you cannot simply enjoy it as entertainment. Also his short story *Benito Cereno*.

From Chris:

- Mary Oliver's poem, "Bone" from her collection *Why I Wake Early*, www.panhala.net/Archive/Bone.html
- Mary Oliver writes mostly about nature, this earth, it's creatures and sometimes human invasion of it. Her voice is that of an observer, yet at the same time she becomes a champion of the subject, telling us so easily of the gifts we receive in every moment, if we are paying attention.

From Joanna:

- Martin Luther King, Jr.'s "I Have a Dream" speech—prophetic poetry if there ever was
- Walter Brueggeman's poetry and his *Prayers for a Privileged People*.
- I also have been shaped by the book *Prayers* by Fr. Michael Quoist.

Walter:

> *The dominant ideology does not want us to come to consciousness. It wants us to be shoppers, spectators and consumers. Because people who become conscious are not easily administered.*

Joanna:

> *Why is the church so susceptible to colluding with that ideology when we should be a counter-cultural institution?*

Walter:

> *The force of the ideology is so powerful and so tantalizing that it takes huge intentionality to resist it. Also we have a long history—many would say since Constantine*—of being allied with imperial power and we scratch each other's backs. My symbol of that is in St. Louis where I lived for many years. Clergy there can still get to Cardinal's games for a dollar. The reason is that when baseball went to Sundays, they were afraid that the church would oppose it. In order to silence the clergy they gave them all a baseball pass. That's just a little thing, but it's all along the line like that. What the leaders of the ideology know is that almost everybody can be bought off.*

Joanna:

> *I remember Martin Luther King saying that we need to be the conscience of the state, not the servant. I think we keep forgetting that.*

Chris:

> *I think it takes real diligent work to be present and conscious. It's hard. You have to do it every day always.*

Ariel:

> *I experience this problem in terms of framing and taboos. There are certain things we are allowed to talk about in church and beyond, and other things which are beyond the pale. Just to notice the obvious and to name it becomes a rather brave act. There are certain things that we are not allowed to talk about; like Martin Luther King not being allowed to talk about poverty and the Vietnam War. There was a little field in which he was allowed to speak, but if he behaved like the citizen he was and spoke out on something that was not in the allowed agenda, then he was killed. A lot of us had the experience of being called traitors just for talking about things that were perfectly obvious—like herds of elephants in the room—but just by mentioning them we got labelled. You have to just keep talking.*

Walter:

> *I think the way that gets said often in the church to the pastor, if the pastor crosses that line, is, "Why don't you stay out of economics and politics and just tend to your religion?" As long as you do that no questions are ever raised.*

Ariel:

So take a razor to all the prophetic chapters and just remove them from the Bible!

* Constantine was Roman Emperor from 306 to 337 CE. He was the first Roman emperor to convert to Christianity. In 313 CE he issued the Edict of Milan which legitimized all religions throughout the empire. Prior to his rule, Christians had been subject to persecution and martyrdom. His conversion marks the beginning of a collaborative relationship between the church and the empire.

If you really understand what is being said here, you may be reeling from the shocking truth of it. Let's imagine that you are in a court such as the prophet Micah describes where God is bringing a case against the people. Here's God's seven accusations:

- You choose to remain unconscious so that you can be easily administered.
- You are a member of a church which readily colludes with the dominant ideology in which it is embedded.
- You gain advantage through your membership in the church and are bought off by those who want the church to remain silenced.
- You have become the servant of the state, not its conscience.
- You see things that need to be named and challenged, but you choose not to speak.
- You have allowed the powers to fence you into religion and out of politics and economics.
- You have cut the words of my prophets out of your Bible and behaved as if they never existed.

How do you respond? Try responding in the first person, that is either beginning the sentence with "I…"or with "We…"

On the other hand, none or few of these accusations may belong to you. You may be able to say, "Not guilty, Holy One." Likely, you find yourself somewhere in between, acknowledging that it takes an exceptional human being to measure up to God's expectations. So it's not about guilt or innocence; it's about "all the little things along the way," the moment-to-moment choices, the commitment to nurture and honour consciousness, the willingness to name the elephants in the room, and the step which takes you beyond ideological fences that want to keep you contained. How will you proceed from this moment?

OPTION 3: WHEN THE ETHICAL MEETS THE ARTISTIC

Walter:

> *I want to make a comment about the interface between the ethical and the artistic. I think the church is preoccupied with ethical matters and that means we choose up sides—liberals and conservatives—and we argue, whereas the artistic asks us just to sit with it and to process it and to be led where we had not thought to go. Ethical questions are obviously very important, but we can move to them too quickly. What the artistic asks us to do is to go way underneath that to ponder what is the truth about us that matters before we make ethical decisions.*

Joanna:

> *That's scary when I think about teaching anti-racism; it's hard for us to listen to the voices and to go deeper, so we want to get past that and say, "I don't want to hear your story any more. I just want to go and fix it. Everything will be all right." It's pretty scary to be in there hearing through the voice of an artist.*

Walter:

> *Because the strategy of fixing it just wants to cover it all over.*

Joanna:

> *I read the poems in Street Vibes—a homeless newspaper. It just amazes me that there are people who are homeless and they are writing poetry. It's a totally different way of communicating what their situation is.*

Walter:

> *So the fantasy I have when the church gathers around Scripture, if it ever gathers around prophetic texts: "Here we all are, taking time to hear this poetry again." Then we immediately close it off by saying, "Praise to you, Lord Christ." Sometimes we shouldn't say that. We should say, "O, wow!" Just let it be. Let it work.*

When have you noticed that tendency for groups within your church to move too quickly to fix things based on an ethical analysis, rather than to welcome the artistic perspective that can take the participants to a deeper understanding of the truth of the issue at hand?

Could you imagine, in the situation presented by Joanna, a group from your church which is addressing issues of homelessness actually taking time to hear the poetry of those who are homeless, or finding a way of visiting with homeless artists and musicians to be touched and challenged by their perspective? How would you go about pursuing something like that where an issue is engaged through an artistic medium rather than through an action-oriented strategy?

When you watched the DVD you heard Alice, Ariel and Joanna reflecting on our alienation from our bodies which shows up in the physical presentation of young women, our relationship with food, our discomfort with parts of the Bible that celebrate human sexuality, the issue of diet in our fast-food culture and the impact on community of our food choices.

Walter Brueggemann offers two reflections in response to these observations:

> *When we cannot talk about our bodies, then we cannot talk about the body politic or care for the body politic. The two are intimately related to each other.*

> *It seems to me that what we're describing in this is a profound sense of alienation from ourselves. I think that the consumer ideology depends upon our being alienated from ourselves and it resists our being in touch with our true bodied selves, because then we wouldn't be susceptible to all this commodity advertising.*

Make a list on newsprint or whiteboard of all the ways that you allow the culture to influence the choices and judgements you make about your bodies.

What would be some ways that you could deny the cultures "hold" on your bodies and live more in touch with your true "bodied" selves?

Offer this prayer:

> We are frightened and flee to certitude.
> We hide our real selves
>   and run from our bodily life
>   into safe mantras of assurance.
> We put all of our wagons in tight circles of certitude,
>   imagining that our life there will be safe and happy.
> But you, in your relentless rule,
>   will not let us flee or hide or pretend.
>
> You are like a thief in the night
>   or like rust that eats away at our pretend world.
> You keep after us in your subversive poetry that pierces all of our denials.
> You are the God of all truth.
>
> In your truthfulness
>   you expose our deathliness;
>   you judge our littleness;
>   you call us out from our self-denying pride.
>
> Give us courage for your truth
>   that will make us free,
>   free for ourselves,
>   free for you in joy and gladness,
>   free for all your children
>   and all your creatures.
>
> *—Walter Brueggemann, Cincinnati, 2011*

SESSION | 5

THE GRIEF OF LOSS AS DIVINE JUDGEMENT

BEFORE OR AFTER THE SESSION

Many participants like to come to the group conversation after considering individually some of the issues that will be raised. Others like to take time following the session to do further processing. The following five reflective activities and questions are intended to open your minds, memories and emotions regarding some aspects of this session's topic. Use the space provided here to note your reflections.

What does it look like for something or someone to be "out of sync" with God? Be attentive for people and things that seem to be aligned with the divine, the sacred, the Holy and others that are not. What makes the difference?

About what are you sad? Pay attention this week for feelings of sadness that well up in you in response to various situations, whether relational, political, social, environmental, communal and so on.

What is it that needs acknowledgement in our culture and in our world before you and I and all those involved can be free to move on?

Watch for anywhere in your community, your nation or your world where a person, a group, an organization is doing the work of the prophetic tradition. What are the marks of prophetic action?

Take time to do the writing involved in Option 2, below, in which you will read about the meaning of the word *woe* as used by the prophets of Israel, and do some writing that will lead you to experience that word more fully and personally.

Play the first part of Session 5 on the DVD (about 18 minutes) in which Walter Brueggemann lays the groundwork for the discussion which is to follow.

Having heard Walter speaking, note now the *four key imperatives* of his presentation:

Go With God or It Won't Last!

If you accept the hypothesis that the destruction of Jerusalem in 587 BCE is really the subject of the whole Old Testament, that means that for 250 years the prophets were anticipating the destruction of Jerusalem. That does not mean they were predicting it or that they knew in a cognitive way that it was going to happen. It means that they knew that *a city and a dynasty and a temple and an economy and an urban infrastructure that are out of sync with God simply cannot be sustained.*

Attend to the Sadness for All That Will Be Lost!

The prophets are an invitation to sadness for impending loss that they know is coming. And because they believe in moral accountability the loss is articulated as divine judgement. I have really come to think that it *is loss over which they are sad.* Abraham Heschel showed us that the prophets essentially talk about God's sadness and God's suffering awareness that *everything that was treasured is going to be lost. It's an invitation to a funeral for the death of everything precious.*

Face What's Happening or Stay Stuck!

Many people now know in their guts, but not yet in their heads, that we are watching the death of our culture. We are watching the end of a certain extravagant economy. We are watching the end of environmental practices that cannot be sustained. We are watching the diminishment of the common good among us; but the ideology of consumerism wants us not to notice, wants us to put the wagons in a row, keep out the problems, keep out the poor people, keep out the need, and imagine that we can sustain life that way in the world. I think that 9/11, the Gulf spill, Katrina and the collapse of the economy are a package of diminishment that requires acknowledgement because *until those things are acknowledged we cannot move on.*

Lead the Way in Speaking Honestly about the Loss!

I believe *it is the work of the prophetic tradition in our society as in that ancient society to cut through the celebration and the affirmations and to invite people to a sustained period of sadness.* I believe that the sadness, when it is unacknowledged, shows up in many destructive ways. It shows up in our anger toward gays and lesbians; it shows up in policies that want to exclude poor people. I suggest that in this ocean of self-indulgence and self-deception, that constitutes our society, *the church might be an arena in which we gather honestly to talk about the loss because the acknowledgement of loss is the only door to newness.*

These four imperatives naturally flow out of Walter Brueggemann's teaching in this session. At this point in the series we really hear Brueggemann's voice resonating with the voices of the prophets. As you listen to him, which of the four imperatives touch most clearly the concerns of your own life and leadership:

• Go with God or it won't last!
• Attend to the sadness for all that will be lost!
• Face what's happening or stay stuck!
• Lead the way in speaking honestly about the loss!

Talk together in the group about the way each of these themes connect with your own life and leadership today.

Now play the rest of Session 5 on the DVD. The group discussion surfaces the issues that will be covered in the rest of your session together. You'll have the opportunity to choose options based on group interest and available time.

Walter leads us into a deep reflection on the significance of the word *woe*. He introduces it in this way:

> *I'm going to spend my time in this segment on one word:* Woe. *Now, very often we take the word* woe, *if we take it at all, as if it were an angry threat-like word as in, "Woe to you!" But that's not right. The word* woe *is not anger or threat. It is sadness. It is a word for a funeral. And so every time the prophets say, "Woe," they say. "Imagine yourself at a death."*

Members of the small group, meeting with him pick up this theme of deep sadness with these thoughts:

Joanna:

> *Your talk almost makes me want to cry.*

Damon:

> *The church needs to step up and call for a national time of woe, a national time of sadness, and not be ashamed to do it.*

Alice:

> *The first time I began to think about grief as a good thing was listening to a former colleague of mine preach at a funeral. I'd been to funerals before but hadn't paid that much attention. Charlie spoke about grief and said we should cry. We know there's the resurrection and that's great and I'll get to that, but it is sad that we have lost this person that we're not going to be able to eat breakfast with tomorrow morning. And it's a good thing to cry for them, to be sad, to*

> *be miserable even, to be filled with woe, to experience that grief in all its depth as a gift. I never really thought about that until then.*

Walter:

> *I think we know a lot about grief. We haven't transposed it into public dimensions. It's work that remains to be done.*

Joanna:

> *I'm not sure that we've transposed it into divine consciousness; the grief of God.*

Walter:

> *All of that requires that God be articulated as a character who's in play and that's already threatening to people. That's what the poets did. God has a complex interior life that the poets probe and that's not what you get in church mainly.*

> *I think there's an overlap between sadness and guilt. And the guilt is real, but it ought not to trump sadness. The first fact is the sense of loss. I may be culpable for that loss so I have to deal with that, but before I do, I've got to be honest about the loss.*

About what do you feel truly sad?

The conversation leads us to a consideration of community grief and loss as people talk about funerals, national acts of mourning, and processes of truth-telling. Where do you see situations that call for communal acts of grieving and acknowledgement of loss? How might your faith community be involved in such initiatives?

What are all the ways you deal with that sadness?

Walter:

I want to cite some "woe" passages and have you sit with them for a while to look at the long-term sadness that these poets know because life out of sync with God is not sustainable.

The first poet-oracle that I cite is in Amos 6:4:

> Woe to you!
> Big trouble to you!
> Loss to you
>> who lounge on beds of ivory,
>> who drink wine at the club from huge bowls,
>> who sing idle songs,
>> who slaughter calves for veal!
> Woe to you in your consumer self-indulgence.
> Woe to you
>> who are not grieved over Israel,
>> who do not see that your society is dying,
>> who really don't care that we're going to hell in a hand basket!
> Therefore, you will be the first to go into exile.

Note that exile is the big threat in the ancient world because what empires always did was to displace people. This kind of upheaval causes people to be displaced: "You will not be able to sustain your comfortable nest of self-indulgence." If you look at that oracle from Amos, God isn't even mentioned. It doesn't say, "God is gonna get you." It just says, "Big trouble is coming."

In Isaiah 5, there's a series of woes; like the poet got on a roll with that and kind of liked the cadences so he just went on with it:

> Woe to you who buy up other people's property so that you own so much land there are no neighbors anymore! There's just you.

Note that he's describing imperialism; he's describing territorial expansion; he's describing the right of eminent domain whereby shopping malls displace poor people's houses for the sake of the economy; he's describing greed.

> Woe to you who live by acquisitive greed!
> Woe to you who get up early to start drinking and then bribe officials so that you can get court rulings.

I wouldn't know how drinking leads to that, but what he's describing is a life that is all wrapped around me and my self-sufficiency—who doesn't care about anybody else.

> Woe to you
>> who call evil good, and good evil,
>> who call bitter sweet, and sweet bitter.
> Woe to you who engage in euphemisms.
> Woe to you who call things by their wrong name.
> Woe to you who cut people out of health care and call it medical reform.
> Woe to you who bomb children and call it collateral damage.

What the poets always know is that huge concentrations of power always have to resort to euphemisms because to call things by their right name is unbearable, and we don't want to talk that way. So imagine that the poets are people who are not confused by the ideology of the day but who cut through to call things by their right name and then imagine that the church is the only place in town where things are called by their right name.

Notice how Brueggemann moves from a rendering of the texts in Amos and Isaiah to a contemporary and personal expression of grief using the "woe" structure. Now it's your turn! Together create your own "woe" rendering of losses you share together. Remember this guidance from Walter: *The word* woe *is not anger or threat. It is sadness. It is a word for a funeral. And so every time the prophets say, "Woe," they say. "Imagine yourself at a death."*

Woe to you who…

Woe to you who…

Woe to you who…

Woe to you who…

Woe to you who…

Of course you can't do this writing without recognizing your own implication in the great sadnesses of our time. We have all participated in economic decisions that have brought suffering to others. We have all used euphemisms to avoid having to name things the way they really are. We have all known nests of self-indulgence. Talk about where you find yourselves in this process of naming losses and sadness. Be clear, and be compassionate both with yourself and with others. Keep in mind Walter's teaching about sadness and guilt:

I think there's an overlap between sadness and guilt. And the guilt is real, but it ought not to trump sadness. The first fact is the sense of loss. I may be culpable for that loss so I have to deal with that, but before I do, I've got to be honest about the loss.

In conversation some members of the group talk about September 11th as an example of a time when it seemed like there was an opportunity for a national "waking up" to expose the ideology of American exceptionalism:

Prince raises this question:

> How are we going to transition from this conscious expression of grief to an action—a different way of behaving? I see a society that experiences these periods of grief almost collectively but then they allow themselves to be pacified again by the ideology of exceptionalism. I don't see us taking this reflection as something that moves us on a new path—something that transforms us. That's where we're really trying to go, trying to be transformed by consciously experiencing the grief. I'm questioning whether or not we can do that.

And Chris responds:

> I think it's amazing that after September 11th happened that that didn't do more than I think it should have done to our country. I don't know what should have happened. I was in Manhattan that day. I remember several days after that, watching television and seeing the people in our government singing, "America the Beautiful'"and thinking to myself, "Wow! We woke up." But I don't think we really did.

Walter reflects:

> I think that big service we had at the national cathedral was a moment when the space could have been opened up, but it was immediately closed in triumphalism.

Later Prince presents the model of the post-Apartheid South African Truth and Reconciliation Commission as an example of societal transformation of the most inspiring kind.

When have you experienced that process of communal waking up, moving from grief and loss to genuine transformation?

What is it that makes it so hard—almost impossible—for a community or nation to do what Nelson Mandela's South Africa did?

OPTION 4: THE WORK OF THE PROPHETIC TRADITION

As we heard earlier in his opening teaching, Walter spoke about the work that the church might engage in to facilitate the processes of societal grieving:

> I believe it is the work of the prophetic tradition in our society to cut through the celebration and the affirmations and to invite people to a sustained period of sadness. I believe that the sadness, when it is unacknowledged, shows up in many destructive ways. I suggest the church might be an arena in which we gather honestly to talk about the loss because the acknowledgement of loss is the only door to newness.

Alice begins to think about ways that she might do this kind of work in her own faith community:

> It seems to me that a lot of this anger and rhetoric that we see in the news is less anger and more grief—that things are not what we thought they were going to be. But that's not what they are saying, of course. Perhaps it falls to us to point those things out. On a very practical level, I might show a clip from some commentator and say, "This folks; this is grief, this is sadness."

Earlier in the DVD we heard Ariel talking about the Holy Week ritual in which she participates in Cincinnati:

> I'm thinking of the stations of the cross in Cincinnati where we walk around to different parts of the ghetto and grieve. If it's done in a way where we really experience it and don't rush into the polemics, but just spend some time feeling it, and feeling that the way we've been doing things just can't continue.

Do you want to be part of the Prophetic Tradition to which Walter is referring? What would it take for you to do that and to feel like you are measuring up to your own expectations of what is required?

Creativity is called for in "*moving the church to be an arena in which we gather honestly to talk about the loss.*" In what ways might you go about this? What leadership is required of you and the other members of this group?

Offer this prayer:

All around us is loss.

Our old world is daily diminished before our very eyes.
We weep over our losses
    the way in which Jesus wept over lost Jerusalem.
We grieve over 9/11
    and the loss of our certitude,
    the expose of our vulnerability,
    the forfeiture of our entitlement,
    the collapse of our security,
    the failure of our privilege.
We are overwhelmed
    about how deep
        and how broad is the loss for those of us
            who have been so well situated
        that we thought "it could never happen here."

The loss causes us to be sad…and angry…and anxious.
And the more we measure
    and calculate
    and feel the threat of newness,
        the deeper is our sadness,
        the wider is our anger,
        the longer is our anxiety.

Envelop us in the tears you must surely shed over our world that is gone.
Give us freedom, amid such loss,
    to stand with you
    as you grace this world with your presence.
You are the Friday God of death.
So give us courage and chutzpah
    to be honest in our grief
    and to reckon that you are in the midst of it
        and perhaps the cause of it.

Receive our grief and go there with us,
    perhaps there to conjure newness for us
that we cannot imagine for ourselves.

                    —*Walter Brueggemann, Cincinnati, 2011*

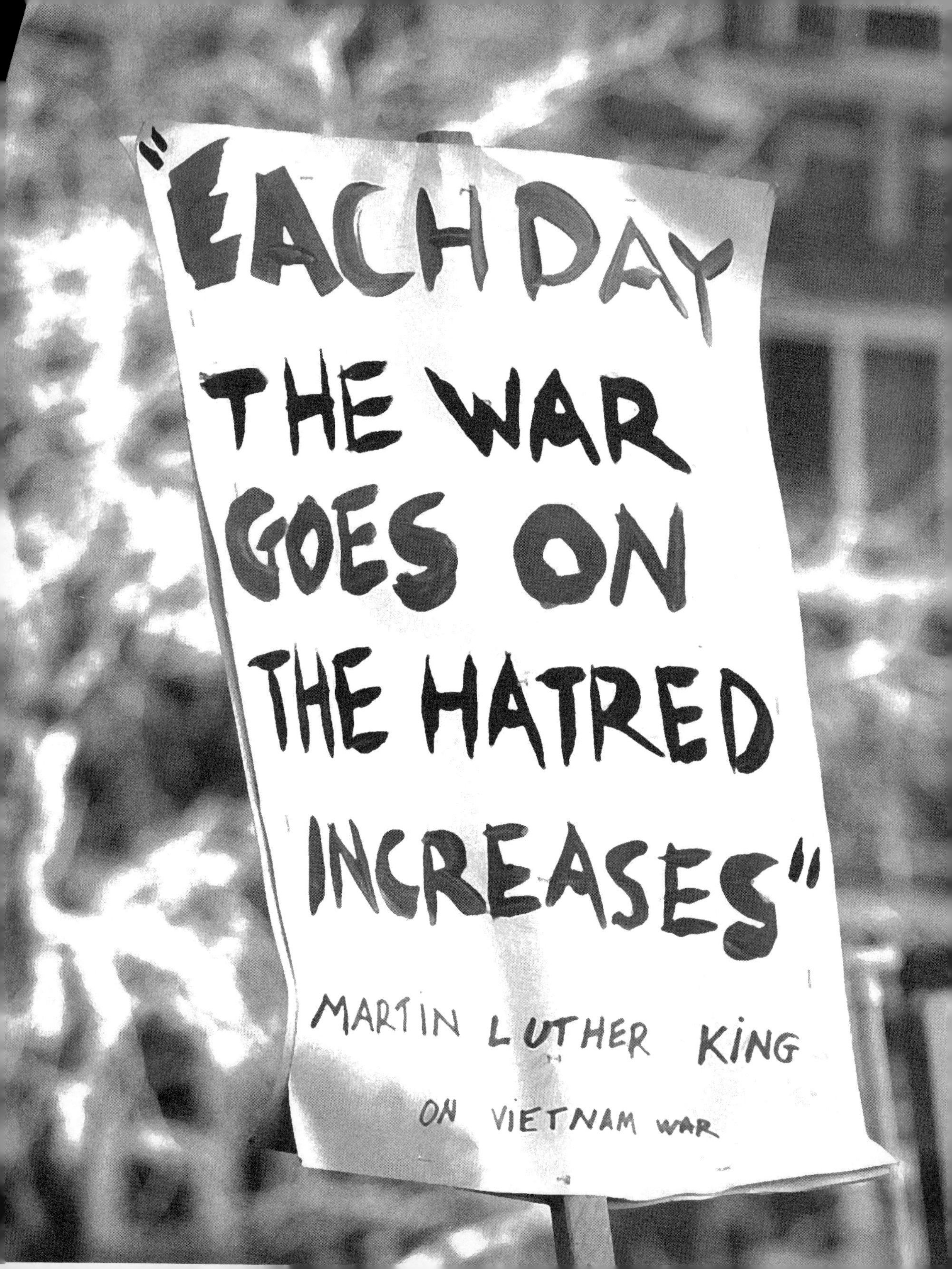
"EACH DAY
THE WAR
GOES ON
THE HATRED
INCREASES"
MARTIN LUTHER KING
ON VIETNAM WAR

SESSION | 6

THE PROMISSORY LANGUAGE THAT BREAKS DESPAIR

BEFORE OR AFTER THE SESSION

Many participants like to come to the group conversation after considering individually some of the issues that will be raised. Others like to take time following the session to do further processing. The following five reflective activities and questions are intended to open your minds, memories and emotions regarding some aspects of this session's topic. Use the space provided here to note your reflections.

Take time on your own to read and reflect on the biblical passages presented in the first part of this session. These passages will be addressed by Walter Brueggemann in his teaching in this session.

The writers of those biblical passages all had a vision of God as One who keeps doing new things in creation. As you anticipate this session, watch out for ways that God is indeed doing new things that are an embodiment of God's Shalom.

What do you find most hard to let go of? What things are you holding on to that you know would be better left behind?

What does God remember about you?

Notice the ways that you are living out the practice of neighborliness this week.

Play the first part of Session 6 of the DVD (about 18 minutes) in which Walter Brueggemann lays the groundwork for the discussion which is to follow.

You'll notice that, unlike his presentation in the other five sessions, Brueggemann has created a Biblical trail for us to follow in this session. He's very clear in his presentation about the significance and meaning of this biblical path, so rather than repeat any of that commentary, we begin this session by hearing the biblical passages to which he was referring, allowing them to live within us and between us in this community of learning.

Go around the circle and have people take it in turn to read and then respond to the questions at the end.

Genesis 18:9-15

[9] They said to him, "Where is your wife Sarah?" And he said, "There, in the tent." [10] Then one said, "I will surely return to you in due season, and your wife Sarah shall have a son." And Sarah was listening at the tent entrance behind him. [11] Now Abraham and Sarah were old, advanced in age; it had ceased to be with Sarah after the manner of women. [12] So Sarah laughed to herself, saying, "After I have grown old, and my husband is old, shall I have pleasure?" [13] The Lord said to Abraham, "Why did Sarah laugh, and say, 'Shall I indeed bear a child, now that I am old?' [14] Is anything too wonderful for the Lord? At the set time I will return to you, in due season, and Sarah shall have a son." [15] But Sarah denied, saying, "I did not laugh"; for she was afraid. He said, "Oh yes, you did laugh."

Isaiah 40:1-2

[1] Comfort, O comfort my people,
    says your God.
[2] Speak tenderly to Jerusalem,
    and cry to her
that she has served her term,
    that her penalty is paid,
    that she has received from the Lord's hand
        double for all her sins.

Isaiah 51:1-2

[1] Listen to me, you that pursue righteousness,
    you that seek the Lord.
Look to the rock from which you were hewn,
    and to the quarry from which
        you were dug.
[2] Look to Abraham your father
    and to Sarah who bore you;
for he was but one when I called him,
    but I blessed him and made him many.

Isaiah 54:1-2

[1] Sing, O barren one who did not bear;
    burst into song and shout,
    you who have not been in labour!
For the children of the desolate woman will
        be more
    than the children of her that is married,
        says the Lord.
[2] Enlarge the site of your tent,
    and let the curtains of your habitations be
        stretched out;
do not hold back; lengthen your cords
    and strengthen your stakes.

Isaiah 65:17-18

[17] For I am about to create new heavens
and a new earth;
the former things shall not be remembered
or come to mind.
[18] But be glad and rejoice for ever
in what I am creating;
for I am about to create Jerusalem as a joy,
and its people as a delight.

Jeremiah 31:31-33

[31] The days are surely coming, says the Lord,
when I will make a new covenant with the
house of Israel and the house of Judah. [32]
It will not be like the covenant that I made
with their ancestors when I took them by
the hand to bring them out of the land of
Egypt—a covenant that they broke, though
I was their husband, says the Lord. [33] But
this is the covenant that I will make with the
house of Israel after those days, says the Lord:
I will put my law within them, and I will
write it on their hearts; and I will be their
God, and they shall be my people.

Ezekiel 44:1-2

[1] Then he brought me back to the outer gate
of the sanctuary, which faces east; and it was
shut. [2] The Lord said to me: This gate shall
remain shut; it shall not be opened, and no
one shall enter by it; for the Lord, the God
of Israel, has entered by it; therefore it shall
remain shut.

Luke 1:46-55

[46] And Mary said,
"My soul magnifies the Lord,
[47] and my spirit rejoices in God
my Saviour,
[48] for he has looked with favour on the
lowliness of his servant.

Surely, from now on all generations will
call me blessed;
[49] for the Mighty One has done great things
for me
and holy is his name.
[50] His mercy is for those who fear him
from generation to generation.
[51] He has shown strength with his arm;
he has scattered the proud in the
thoughts of their hearts.
[52] He has brought down the powerful from
their thrones,
and lifted up the lowly;
[53] he has filled the hungry with good things,
and sent the rich away empty.
[54] He has helped his servant Israel,
in remembrance of his mercy,
[55] according to the promise he made to our
ancestors,
to Abraham and to his descendants for
ever."

Luke 13:11-13, 16

[11] And just then there appeared a woman
with a spirit that had crippled her for
eighteen years. She was bent over and was
quite unable to stand up straight.
[12] When Jesus saw her, he called her over
and said, "Woman, you are set free from
your ailment." [13] When he laid his hands on
her, immediately she stood up straight and
began praising God…[16] "And ought not this
woman, a daughter of Abraham whom Satan
bound for eighteen long years, be set free
from this bondage?"

Luke 19:9-10

[9] Then Jesus said to [Zacchaeus], "Today
salvation has come to this house, because
he too is a son of Abraham. [10] For the Son
of Man came to seek out and to save the
lost."

Revelation 22:1-2, 6-7

¹ Then the angel showed me the river of the water of life, bright as crystal, flowing from the throne of God and of the Lamb ² through the middle of the street of the city. On either side of the river is the tree of life with its twelve kinds of fruit, producing its fruit each month; and the leaves of the tree are for the healing of the nations.

⁶ And he said to me, "These words are trustworthy and true, for the Lord, the God of the spirits of the prophets, has sent his angel to show his servants what must soon take place."

⁷ "See, I am coming soon! Blessed is the one who keeps the words of the prophecy of this book."

What's the impact on you of hearing this sequence of texts selected by Walter Brueggemann?

In the previous sessions we were focused on prophetic challenge, moral coherence, human denial and the grief of loss. Now we come to a session that is all about promise, vision, dream and hope for the future. What's it like to turn that corner so dramatically?

Now play the rest of Session 6 on the DVD. The group discussion surfaces the issues that will be covered in the rest of your session together. You'll have the opportunity to choose options based on group interest and available time.

Walter:

I think that in a society of defeat and despair such as the one in which we live, that for the prophetic imagination to be opening up our world of dreaming possibility for what God is going to do next is a really important mandate. In the end, the prophets are not preoccupied with judgement or with sadness or with grief or with loss; they are preoccupied with God's resolve to do something new that will be an embodiment of God's Shalom.

The question that is always before the people of God is whether God can do something beyond our shut-down possibilities. This seems to me to be an enormously important poetic prophetic act now in our society, because we are at the end of so many things that the question of faith now is really can and will God do something new that will make our life safe and joyous, healthy and human. And so what I like to think is that all of these poetic promises are really anticipations of Martin (Luther King) when he said, "I have a dream." I have a dream of a new Jerusalem. I have a dream of a new temple. I have a dream of a new covenant. And history is simply the working out of that dream.

I continue to be dazzled by the generative capacity of this very lean minority voice that keeps sounding through our history. It gives me chill bumps to think that we could be a part of that ongoing witness that's against the grain.

Alice:

I've read somewhere about the Christian faith being about participating in God's dream; that in creation God had a dream for what this could be and that we are fully awake when we are participating in that dream and when we are dreaming together. In his book Love Wins, *Rob Bell talks about how God is so excited about making new things, so excited about possibilities, that God didn't just make us, God made things that can make more things. So when we are part of that creativity we are truly part of that dream that God has.*

How could you develop and encourage prophetic imagination within your community, that is, *the capacity for dreaming the possibility of what God is going to do next?*

OPTION 2: MAKING SPACE FOR IDENTITY AND IMAGINATION

What do you make of Walter's statement that he gets *chill bumps when he thinks that we could be a part of that ongoing witness that's against the grain?*

Walter:

[Speaking about the Jewish community after the destruction of Jerusalem:] Two things happened to the faithful Jews. One thing— they knew they could not go back to the way it used to be. That's huge. The second thing is that they discovered that they did not belong to the empire, but that they had to act out of their peculiar Jewish identity. Sometimes when I process with myself I can get one or other of those: if I think I can't go back then I think I'll just settle for the empire; or if I think I don't want to be in the empire,

I'll just go back. When I see that I can't do either one of those, I create space in which I am not only able to do something new, but I am required to do something new.

One of the things I understand, if I understand Martin Luther King's speech on dream correctly, is that he had no plan or blueprint about how to enact that dream. I think that with out moral earnestness in the church we are often wanting to be practical and pragmatic about how we are going to do this: a "to do" list. That's not unimportant but there has to be space around that for you just to imagine beyond the things that we know how to do.

I think that this imagination opens up the space of possibility that we then have to occupy. I think that if we don't have inventive imagination then we don't have any room in which to act in new responsible ways.

Ariel:

The parts of the prophets that always speak to me are the parts where it says "I knew who you were and I had your name written on my hand before you were even conceived." So it seems to me that part of the solution is remembering who we are and whose we are.

Walter:

And we remember who they are because God remembers who we are.

Ariel:

We're heading off into something that seems like a wilderness, and we're having to be unencumbered so the travelling advice was just take what you can carry and travel light. So we're getting disencumbered of a lot of baggage, and we're putting on our tough shoes, and we're heading out into unfamiliar territory, but we're receptive. We remember who we are, and that's almost enough baggage to sustain us.

How will you as a community ensure that there is always time for acts of imagination and possibility that carry you beyond the old familiar ways into radical and transformative ways of being God's people?

Like the Jewish community after the destruction of Jerusalem, you can't go back to the way it used to be, and you have discovered that you have a peculiar identity that is outside the identity of empire. What is your identity as a community if it is not of the dominant culture, the empire of this time?

What does God remember about you?

OPTION 3: LETTING GO IN ORDER TO MOVE ON

Letting go in order to move on with freedom and spaciousness is an aspect of option 2, but we are choosing to treat it separately because the inability and unwillingness to relinquish what has come before is one of the most significant things that keeps us from moving boldly into the future.

Walter:

> I don't think that this new wave of poetry could happen until they had gotten clear that they had to relinquish what was gone. As long as you keep wishing to have back what was gone, you're probably blocked from dreaming about something else.

> I agree with you about giving up material things, but I suspect it also means to give up some of our angers, to give up some of our hates, to give up some of our fears, to give up some of our stereotypes, to give up, as Paul says in Colossians, to give up those dimensions of the old self.

Alice:

> Dreaming a future rather than complaining about the past. We do that a lot in the church! "We've never done it that way before!" Why start now?

Joanna:

> I also think it means to give up our sense of limits, because I think that God goes beyond those limits, and what we think is possible is not what God thinks is possible. That's what I think of as being given license to dream or license to imagine: we aren't bound by what we think is possible.

Make a list on newsprint of all the things that you know you have to relinquish to free you as a community to move forward. Another way to ask it is to follow Paul's thinking and to ask about the dimensions of the "old self" that need to be released. Make sure that you respond to this not only as individuals but also as a faith community that has a tendency to hang on to those things that are familiar and safe.

Joanna suggests that we also need to give up our sense of limits and live into God's limitless possibilities. What limits are you still holding on to?

OPTION 4: IMAGING THE UNKNOWN FUTURE

Walter:

What you can see in these exilic prophets then is that every prophet filters that unknown future through their own lens of experience. So Isaiah—who is this urban guy—he imagines that the future will be a new Jerusalem... Jeremiah—who is a child of Deuteronomy and the Covenant of Torah—talks about a new covenant like the covenant of Sinai that has been broken... Ezekiel— whose a big steeple church pastor in Jerusalem—imagines the future as a new temple... So you get a new city. You get a new temple. You get a new covenant. You get a new possibility.

Joanna:

When you talk about a new heaven and a new earth as a new Jerusalem, I start to imagine a new Cincinnati and what that would look like. Actually I see with that diversity you are talking about; a new Cincinnati would be one that embraces the whole diversity of people here so that Cincinnati is not comprised of just high-end condos and people with water-views, but it embraces all the people, rich and poor, black and white, who live here. And we could celebrate that.

Trying to imagine a new Cincinnati the same way that the biblical authors thought about a new Jerusalem and being able to dream that in a way sometimes takes us out of the realm of possibility but then at least we can picture what it can be.

How do you speak of the unknown future? What 21st-century metaphors and images will you use in speaking imaginatively, forcefully and inspiringly about God's emerging future?

Perhaps there are other contemporary writers, poets and prophets whose holy imaginative language lures you into the future? Can you name some of these?

Walter:

> *I've come to think that neighborliness happens face-to-face as well as in terms of policy formation and all along the line between those two things.*

Chris:

> *Neighborliness is bravery.*

Walter:

> *That's right.*

Chris:

> *It's very simple I think. We do the simple things.*

Walter:

> *But it's very counter-cultural.*

The word *neighborliness* has come up a few times in this series as a word to represent the living out of God's compassion and God's passion for justice in our relationships and in our world. The conversation here suggests that neighborliness takes bravery, yet it is simple—and it is counter-cultural. In what ways are you seeing the consistent practice of neighborliness in your community as a way of opening space and asserting identity of the kind that Walter has been speaking about?

As you conclude this series of six sessions, spend time together discussing what's next for you—individually, as the small community you've become, as members of the churches to which you return…

Offer this prayer:

> You are the God of all things new.
> You lurk on Saturday night in silence
> > just as you lurked
> > > at the edge of that old deportation.
> And then you leapt up on Easter morning with new life,
> > just as you enunciated homecoming for our ancient people.
>
> You refuse the power of death
> and have broken open our displacement with new possibility.
>
> We give thanks for your promises you have kept among us,
> > and for your promises still under way,
> > > promises of a new heaven,
> > > > a new earth,
> > > > a new Jerusalem, and
> > > > a new covenant.
>
> We watch with eager longing
> > for your newness
> > > that will outrun all our losses.
>
> Emancipate us from our anxiety to watch for your gifts of newness
> > and to receive the strange forms
> > > that your new beginnings may take among us.
>
> At the far edge of our exile,
> > just as the new day breaks,
> > we will shout with glad elation,
> "He is risen indeed."

—Walter Brueggemann, Cincinnati, 2011

Walter Brueggemann

Tim Scorer

Notes

Notes

Notes

Notes

Notes